CARING F ~~⌐⌐⌐~~ GERBIL

How to care for your Gerbil and everything you need to know to keep them well

WRITTEN BY VETERINARY EXPERT

DR. GORDON ROBERTS BVSC MRCVS

Hello! My name is Gordon Roberts and I'm the author of this book. I hope you enjoy all of the specialist advice it contains. I'm a huge advocate of preventative care for animals, and I'd love to see more pet owners taking the time to research their pet's health care needs.

Being proactive and educating yourself about your pet's health now, rather than later on, could save you and your pet a lot of trouble in the long run.

If you'd like to read more of my professional pet care advice simply go to my website at http://drgordonroberts.com/freereportsdownload/.

As a thank you for purchasing this book, you'll find dozens of bonus pet care reports there to download and keep, absolutely free of charge!

Best wishes,

Gordon
Founder, Wellpets

Contents

~

Introduction

Have you decided you want gerbils in your life? You're not alone. Around the world, thousands if not millions of people are keeping these cute creatures as pets. Not only are they small and adorable with their almond shaped eyes and furry tails, they're also great fun for children, and don't take up a lot of space in the home. This doesn't mean that they're low maintenance though; if you want to own one of these little pets, you're going to need to prepare yourself for the work that comes along with it. Cages need to be cleaned regularly, food and bedding need to be bought, and the gerbil is going to need lots of TLC from you on a daily basis. Once you're ready to take on these responsibilities, this book will guide you through the journey of looking after your first gerbil. Hold on tight – it's going to be a fun ride!

Chapter 1:
About the Gerbil

Gerbils are no ordinary pet. They have their own unique biology and characteristics – not to mention a cheeky, endearing personality which sets them apart. Before you decide to take a gerbil home, read this chapter to find out what makes these pets so different from other rodents, and why they are so popular with people who love small animals.

What are gerbils?

Put simply, gerbils belong to the rodent family, which means that they are closely related to small whiskered animals like the mouse and the vole. The word "rodent" comes from the latin word rodere which means "to gnaw". All rodents have one thing in common: a set of front teeth (known as incisors) on the top and bottom jaws, which grow throughout the animal's life.

Rodents make up about 40% of all mammals on earth, making them one of nature's most successful creatures. They are one of the most diverse species, with some living in trees, some being semi-aquatic and some even thriving in human habitats. With these impressive biological credentials, the gerbil is not just a common house pet – he is a creature with wild and fascinating origins.

What sets gerbils apart?

Gerbils are often confused with other small rodent pets like the mouse and the rat. Whilst gerbils are a similar size to some of these creatures, they come from different habitats and have different biological characteristics. For example:

The gerbil is the same size as a mouse, but has a much longer tail and a very different face shape. The eyes tend to be larger and the nose is more pointed.

Unlike mice, gerbils tend to stand up on their hind legs to look around, which gives them almost squirrel-like characteristics
The gerbil has a long tail just like a mouse or rat, but the gerbil's tail is covered with fur, rather than skin, and has a tufty part at the end

Types of gerbils

There are thought to be around 100 different gerbil breeds around the world, and each type can be found in its own habitat in the Indian, African and Asian deserts. Astonishingly, only two types of gerbil are actually kept as pets – the rest of the gerbil population are found only in the wild. These two pet breeds are the Mongolian gerbil and the fat tailed gerbil.

The fat tailed gerbil

These gerbils have only recently been kept as pets, so you may not find them in your local pet shop just yet. They are smaller than the typical gerbil, and have four lower teeth instead of the usual six found in other gerbil varieties. The most noticeable difference in these gerbils is their fatter, club shaped tails which are pink and much shorter than the tails of other gerbil breeds. These tails disguise a clever adaptation; they can retain water and fats just like a camel's hump. This makes them very well suited to desert environments where water and food are scarce. There are a lot of varied opinions on these gerbils as pets, mainly because they are only newly domesticated. For example, some fat tailed gerbil owners say they are very docile compared to other gerbil types, but some people say they are more nippy because of their smaller size. Because we still know comparatively little about this gerbil variety, it may not be the best option for first time gerbil owners. The Mongolian gerbil is a much more reliable pet to keep.

The Mongolian gerbil

The Mongolian gerbil (also known as the "clawed jird") is the classic gerbil type that you will see in pet shops and in books. These gerbils win themselves many fans due to their charismatic natures and their adorable behaviour. They are one of the newest small animals to the pet market. They were first domesticated in 1935, when a group of 20 breeding pairs of gerbils were captured in Mongolia and brought back to Japan for breeding. Later on in 1954, gerbils were sent over to America where they were used as laboratory animals, and a decade later they found their way to the UK.

The scientists that observed them made some astute observations about them, and realised that there was far more to these little creatures than meets the eye. Their endearing, sociable natures eventually led to them being kept as pets. In the UK especially, they quickly became a favourite amongst breeders, who set about breeding different colour varieties and even organising gerbil shows where these new varieties could be exhibited. So began the world's love affair with gerbils. Today, gerbils can be found in pet shops all over the world and the amazing thing is that they are all descended from those first breeding pairs brought to Japan in 1935.

Chapter 2:
Gerbil biology and behaviour

In the last chapter, we learned a little bit about the gerbil's origins and what makes them different from other small pets. Now, we're going to explore some important things to know about the gerbil's biology and its behaviour.

This will help you to understand your gerbil better and to be a more knowledgeable gerbil owner once the time comes to take home your new pet.

How big do gerbils grow?

Most gerbils measure about eight inches long from the tip of the nose to the end of the tail. Their bodies are usually about four inches long once fully grown, with a four inch long tail in addition.

How long do gerbils live?

Gerbils typically live for between two and four years, and very well looked after gerbils can sometimes live to be five years old.

The gerbil's sleep cycle

The gerbil isn't nocturnal (awake only at night). Nor is it diurnal (awake only during the day) like a lot of mammals. Rather, the gerbil lives a life of fancy where it sleeps and wakes intermittently throughout a 24 hour period, which we call being "crepuscular". Experts have noted that gerbils are at their most active at midnight and midday. This sounds a bit chaotic, but it simply means that your gerbil takes a series of naps rather than spending several hours sleeping in a row. It is great for those of us who have busy lifestyles – we don't need to worry about waking up our gerbils at the wrong time, or disturbing their natural sleep cycles, which is often a worry with other pets.

Gerbils and companionship

Gerbils are very sociable creatures and love to live with other gerbils of the same sex and breed. In the wild, they mate for life and the male gerbil will even help with raising the babies. Living in groups allows them to stay safe as there are plenty of eyes watching out for predators. It is also much warmer for them to share burrows with their companions in the harsh Mongolian climate, where night time temperatures can be very low.

With this in mind, you should consider getting gerbils in a pair, as they will be much happier and more comfortable with a companion.

Gerbil activities

Here are some of the behaviours you'll often observe in gerbils:

Chewing

One of the gerbil's favourite activities is chewing. Like gerbils and other rodents, they have teeth which are always growing, and they need to gnaw on hard materials like wood in order to keep the teeth the right length. Overgrown teeth could pose a huge problem for gerbils as the teeth can grow so long that they stop them from eating. So, seeing your gerbil chewing or gnawing away in their cage is a good thing, and will prevent these issues.

Burrowing

Gerbils in the wild burrow deep into the soil to make their homes. Your pet gerbil will usually burrow as much as possible in its tank or cage, and you will need to provide the right environment for it to do this.

Grooming

Gerbils love to groom themselves. As a bonding activity, they also groom their companions which is cute to watch.

Boxing and wrestling

Sometimes you will see two male gerbils having a boxing match, where they stand on their hind legs and hit out at each other with the two front paws. This is natural behaviour which is done to compete for dominance within the pack or colony. If you notice your gerbils doing this, there is usually nothing to worry about unless things get vocal and become too aggressive, progressing into chasing, wrestling and a full blown tussle. If this is the case, you may need to separate the sparring gerbils into their own cages. However, as long as your gerbils are siblings that have lived together from a young age, there should be no problems in this department.

Thumping

Gerbils that feel they are in danger will thump on the ground with their feet to signal to the other gerbils in the colony that there is a predator approaching. Rabbits also do this in the wild, but with just one foot. Usually a pet gerbil will only do this if they smell or sense something unusual – for example a stranger, or another animal near-by. When one gerbil thumps, all of the other gerbils in the colony will run for cover.

Burying food

Like their cousins, gerbils like to hoard their food, burying tasty mor-sels in their burrows to eat at a later date. This means you have to be a bit more careful about cleaning away old food, which can quickly go off in the cage. This old food can quickly build up, so make sure you give treats sparingly.

Scent marking

Gerbils have special scent glands on their bellies, which they can rub along the ground to mark out their scent. In a wild gerbil colony a male will do this to mark out his territory. You might see your pet ger-bil trying to mount another gerbil in the cage – they are just trying to mark their scent on the other gerbil as an act of subordination. You need to keep an eye on this behaviour as it could lead to fighting if it gets out of control.

Eating faeces

It is perfectly normal for gerbils, mice, rabbits and other small pets to eat their own faeces. Younger gerbils do this a lot because it helps their digestive tracts to produce vitamin B12.

Greeting each other

Gerbils greet each other with a quick kiss of the noses, and it's thought that this transmits messages like their gender or age through the saliva.

Winking

It's not uncommon to see a gerbil winking one eye as it munches on a tasty treat you have given it. This winking is also a signal of submission to more dominant members of the group, and another form of greeting.

The personality of the gerbil

Gerbils are a little bit bolder than their cousins. They love to investigate new scents and new people. In fact, the first scientists that worked with gerbils noted that they were too curious to be used for the usual cognitive experiments where lab animals are put into mazes. The gerbil simply has a mind of its own. These days, very few animals in laboratories are gerbils – gerbils have managed to charm their way into our homes instead!

Chapter 3:
Preparing for your gerbils

Now that you know enough about the gerbil to choose one for a pet, it's time to make some preparations for becoming a gerbil owner. This section will go through all the things you need to have ready before bringing home your new pet or pets.

Before the final decision

When it comes to bringing a new pet into your life, you need to ab-solutely sure that you are making the right decision, and that you can commit to looking after this small, vulnerable creature.

So, before you rush out and invest in all the gerbil equipment mentioned in this chapter, make sure you can answer all of the following questions:

- Do I have any other commitments which might prevent me from looking after a gerbil? For example, do I have a new baby arriving, or other pets which might already pose a big enough task to look after?
- Am I sure that there will be someone to look after my gerbil if I go on holiday?
- Do I have the money for all the gerbil food and equipment that I need to invest in?
- Do I have a suitable home for a gerbil, with space away from larger pets and noisy environments?

Are your children old enough for a gerbil?

Over the years, the gerbil has slowly gained a reputation as a children's pet, and they are usually given as a first pet to kids who may be asking for something bigger and more costly such as a puppy. Whilst gerbils make fantastic first-time pets for children, you need to be aware that they are small, fragile and can easily go missing if they escape or are allowed to roam free.

Children should first be educated on how to handle a gerbil and what is acceptable behaviour with these small creatures. For example, a child needs to be very calm when handling a gerbil or they will get nipped, which may result in them dropping and possibly injuring the gerbil. Once the gerbil drops to the ground he will most certainly run for the nearest hiding place, and can then take hours to capture again. So, very young children are not suitable for gerbils. A child over eight or nine years old will be a better candidate, since they will have learned a little bit more about animals, and how to treat them.

Can you commit to looking after a gerbil?

Even if your kids lose interest in the gerbil, you must be there to clean the cage and feed it. Gerbils aren't low maintenance – they need attention and care to make sure they live healthy, happy lives. Cages especially can start to smell if left for too long, and your gerbil is sure to fall ill if he is left more than a week in a dirty cage. So, be prepared for these aspects of gerbil care. You'll also need to invest in bedding, food, and veterinary treatment whenever it's needed.

What you'll need to keep a gerbil

Now that the serious questions have been taken care of, it's time to go out and buy all the equipment you need to keep gerbils. It is much better to make sure you already have all of these items before you bring your gerbils home. It will make everything easier on the big day. Here are the items you will need:

A suitable home for the gerbils

The biggest expense involved in buying gerbils for the first time is, of course, the cage or tank that you're going to keep them in. Don't just buy the first one you come across; spend some time weighing up the pros and cons of each type of housing, for both you and your future pets. For example, some cages are a lot easier to clean out than others. Some cages are much more appealing for gerbils to live in than others. This is a big decision, so choose wisely.

If your pet shop isn't very well stocked, there are lots of pet supply retailers online that will have a wide variety of cages (some may even have reviews from other gerbil owners). Here are some tips for making the right choice:

Avoid gerbil type cages which are totally unsuitable for gerbils. A gerbil will be quite frustrated and unhappy in a gerbil cage with metal bars, as they aren't deep enough to burrow in. A gerbil will be quite frustrated and unhappy in a gerbil cage with metal bars.

Choose something similar to the cage that your gerbils grew up in (unless it was completely unsuitable). In general, if a gerbil was raised in a burrowing environment then it will grow up with a strong desire to burrow – and vice versa.

Plastic tanks are lightweight and easy to lift and clean out, but the plastic itself will not keep its pristine condition for long; it will get scratched and even chewed at.

Rotastack style homes with plastic tubes leading to different chambers can be fun, but the plastic element leaves them vulnerable to being chewed, and they will only ever be a crude imitation of the natural burrows a gerbil would make in the wild.

Glass tanks are good because they are long lasting, durable, escape proof and provide a nice deep environment for digging.

The more gerbils you are keeping, the larger their home will need to be. So, make sure the tank you choose is a good size. There is no such thing as a tank that is too large, but one that is too small will not give your gerbils a happy life, especially if there are several gerbils in your colony. In general, a 10 gallon tank is big enough for two gerbils and you should add on another 5 gallons with each additional gerbil.

Accessories for the gerbil's home

Once you have sourced a suitable home for the gerbils, you need to fill it with the right accessories and equipment, including:

Food bowl

Get a good ceramic food bowl that your gerbil can't tip over or chew to pieces. Ceramic is very hygienic and will last a long time too.

Water bottle or water bowl

Water bowls tend to get dirty or get tipped over easily, so they should really only be used if your gerbil refuses to use a water bottle. You could start off with both a bowl and a bottle to see which one your gerbil prefers.

Something to gnaw on

Gerbils have teeth that grow continuously, and they need to file them down by chewing and gnawing on something hard. There are a few types of gerbil chews ranging from wooden to stone – it's best to get something from the pet shop that's designed specifically for gerbils. Many people want to get a tree branch from their gardens, but there are no guarantees that a tree is free from bacteria and insects, so stick with the pet shop where possible.

A nesting box

Gerbils love to curl up in nests where they feel safe and cosy. Choose an enclosed nesting box for your gerbils with plenty of room for them to turn around and store food in. Fill it with shredded tissue paper or a suitably soft, safe and comfortable bedding.

An exercise wheel

If your cage doesn't come with a wheel, buy one separately. You can get wheels that are stand-alone and don't need to be fixed to bars. Gerbils do a lot of running in the wild and are still only relatively new to being kept as pets. They need to run for a few hours every night. Make sure the wheel you choose is good quality and won't squeak or rattle in the middle of the night.

Toys

You can put some toys in the tank for your gerbils to play with, such as cardboard tubes which make great hiding places. If your pet shop has special kiln dried tree branches (this removes all mould and bacteria) then you should get one as your gerbils will adore having a climbing tree in their tank. Ceramic and wood are much better materials for toys than plastic, which can splinter when chewed and be accidentally ingested. Don't clutter your cage too much with toys though – your gerbils still need a bit of open space to run about. Consider also getting a small bowl and filling it with chinchilla dust – desert rodents love to have a "bath" in the dust in order to clean their fur.

An exercise ball

One great invention for those who don't want their gerbils running free throughout the house is an exercise ball. Your gerbil can still have that feeling of running large distances as he would on his wheel, but he'll also be able to see where he is going and move about your living room floor from the safety of this transparent ball.

A carry case

For trips to the vet, you may want to invest in a small carry case or box. Cardboard shoe boxes can be used, but be warned that gerbils will easily and quickly chew through the cardboard.

Choosing the right substrate for your gerbils

The "substrate" is the material you use to fill your gerbil's tank, in which gerbils will burrow to their heart's content. You need to be very careful about the material you choose for this, as some materials are simply not safe for your little pets.

Here are some tips:
- Shredded cardboard and paper options are usually safe as long as they aren't scented or coloured newspaper ink should be avoided.
- Avoid cat litter which is unsuitable for gerbils
- Avoid wood based litter
- Make sure you choose bedding and substrates that are free from chemicals, dyes and artificial odours; all bedding must be as natural as possible
- Make sure any nest bedding is safe for your gerbil to ingest
- Wherever possible, choose bedding materials that have been made specifically for gerbils, rather than any other pets.

nce you have purchased your checklist of items, the only thing left to do is to choose your gerbil or gerbils. This section has some useful advice for choosing healthy gerbils and making sure you come home with the right pets for you.

Should you buy one gerbil or several?

Although we have mentioned gerbil as a singular quite a lot here, you should never buy a single gerbil as it will be very unhappy living alone. The RSPCA recommends getting same-sex pairs or small groups to start off with. Adult gerbils that have never met should not be housed with each other and will probably fight. It is not a good idea to try and introduce new gerbils to a colony that has already been established – the newcomer is likely to be met with aggression.

It isn't fair to put the gerbils through the stress of a stranger, just because you feel like getting another gerbil. With that in mind, young siblings of the same gender are the best option.

Where to get your gerbils

Now that you've thought through all of the above, it's safe to say that if you're still reading this, you are serious about getting gerbils. Congratulations! The fun is only just beginning. Here are some places you can usually get gerbils from:

Breeders

Before you run off to your local pet shop, do a little bit of research to see if there are any breeders in your area. Gerbils born and raised in family homes will usually be a lot calmer and tamer than gerbils who have been raised in the impersonal setting of a pet shop. The babies will have been handled from a young age, and should be friendlier than those that have had no human contact before. Make sure any breeder you consider can provide you with a reference from someone who has owned one of their gerbils.

They should also be able to tell you all about your chosen gerbils' breed and bloodline. If they can't tell you very much, they are probably an amateur breeder and you need to be especially vigilant in making sure their gerbils are healthy. Ask to see the babies with the mother if possible, or if they have already been weaned, ask if you can see the mother anyway just to check she is well looked after.

In most cases, she will be but it pays to be sure. Since there is little profit to be gained from breeding gerbils, people usually do it for the love of the animals, so you won't find as many "bad" breeders as you would with, say, puppies for example.

Pet shops

Pet shops need to be approached with caution. You should pay a few visits to a pet shop over time to check on how the gerbils there are treated.

For example, are they left out in draughty places? Are their cages cleaned regularly? Do any of them seem to be ill? Are they provided with enough space to move about in, and an exercise wheel? Do the staff know where the gerbils came from – were they bred in the pet shop or have they arrived from an outside breeder?

Bear in mind that a gerbil from a pet shop may not always have had close contact with humans, so you may need to put in some extra work taming it once you get it home. Also, some of the more unscrupulous pet shops forget to wean their gerbils at the right time and as a result, you could end up taking home a female that has already fallen pregnant. Be sure to ask about all this before you make a purchase.

Pet shelters

If you're keen to rehome gerbils that have been abandoned or surrendered, then check your local pet shelter to see if they have gerbils. The advantage of these "pre-loved" gerbils is that they may already be tamed. You will also be doing a good deed by rehoming a gerbil colony that really needs a loving family. Gerbils from pet shelters will have been checked over by a vet to make sure they are healthy enough to be re-homed, which is another advantage for you.

Choosing the right gerbils from a litter

Now comes the fun part: choosing the right gerbils from a litter of pups. Here are some tips:

What to look for...
- Gerbils with bright eyes
- Gerbils that are active and agile

- Gerbils with a healthy appetite
- Gerbils that move well, with no problems with limping or moving in general
- Check that the gerbils you have your eye on are fully weaned, meaning that they are old enough to eat solid food and be away from the mother

What to avoid...
- A gerbil that seems to be scratching a lot on one spot of skin
- A gerbil with dull looking or sunken eyes
- Gerbils with runny faeces or faeces hanging from their fur
- Gerbils with signs of discharge coming from the nose, eyes or rear end, or signs of sneezing, wheezing or coughing
- Check that the gerbils, if old enough to reproduce, have not been living with gerbils of the opposite sex and are not pregnant as a result
- Gerbils with missing hair on their tails – this could either be due to over-grooming by a bored or stressed gerbil, or else it could be a sign of mites.
- Look out for gerbils with tilted heads or that spin in circles – this means there is a problem with the gerbil's ear which has affected its balance
- Look out for gerbils with kinks in their tails – this is a sign of in-breeding, which causes defects.

Should you get males or females?

It is entirely up to you whether you choose to keep male gerbils or female gerbils. However, lots of people say that males are slightly calmer and more docile, and are also a bit larger making them easier to handle. Males will play fight occasionally, but if they are siblings that have always been together they will not fight properly and should get on fine. Females, on the other hand, are said to be a bit more active and curious than their male counterparts, and will want to explore their surroundings rather than sit still. Despite these differences, all gerbils are individuals with their own unique personalities, so it's important not to make too many generalisations.

The big day has arrived! It's time to go and collect your new pets. This section will give you some tips for the first few days of owning your gerbils.

Transporting your gerbil

Your little gerbils are probably going to be stressed when making the journey from where they were raised to your home. To make things easier, you need to transport them in a safe, comfortable container. It should have:

Air holes for breathing

A durable material, preferably not cardboard which can easily get soiled or chewed during the journey. Some soft, cosy bedding to make the journey comfortable. Ideally, some bedding that was originally in your gerbil's old enclosure, so that they have something that smells familiar around them for the first couple of days (you can take this and put it in the new nesting box when you get home).

Arriving home

Ask your pet shop or breeder to provide you with some of the same food your gerbils have been eating all along, so that you don't have to abruptly switch their diet to something new on top of all the other new changes in their environment. Once you get home, place the container inside the tank and letyour gerbils to walk out of it into the cage by themselves, if you can. This will minimise an already stressful situation by not forcing them to be handled just yet.

Make sure your gerbils' housing is in a suitable area of the house. That means somewhere that:
- Is away from draughts and direct sunlight
- Is inaccessible to other pets, whose smells can be very stressful to gerbils
- Is peaceful so that the gerbils can enjoy their naps
- Won't wake anyone up at night, when the gerbils might be running on the wheel

The first three days

Most experts advise waiting a full three days before you try to handle your new gerbils. This gives them time to get used to the new cage and to all the smells and sensations of your home without the stress of also being handled by someone new.

Remember, if you're switching your gerbils from an existing diet to the food you're planning to feed long term, you need to do it gradually to avoid upsetting their stomachs and stressing them out. Mix the new food in a little more each day, and after about a week they should be eating only the new diet.

Chapter 6:
Taming and handling your gerbils

Once your little friends have settled into their new home environment, you can start the process of getting them used to being handled. Some people may be lucky enough to get a gerbil that has already been tamed. If this is the case, you'll just need to get each gerbil used to your smell. Usually though, a new gerbil will need at least a little bit of careful taming before he gets really used to being handled. This section will help you to do that.

Taming and handling individuals

Handling is one of the few activities that need to be done on each individual gerbil. Trying to do this for all gerbils at once will only lead to trouble. So, take each stage slowly and make sure you can tell your gerbils apart, otherwise you will end up with one tame gerbil and one timid one.

Being persistent

Before you begin trying to handle a new gerbil, make sure your expectations are realistic. Not every gerbil is going to enjoy being handled, but they will grow to tolerate it and pretty soon, they won't bat an eyelid. Some gerbils take longer to become tame than others. Dwarf gerbils in particular are a little bit nervous and can nip. Don't let that put you off. A few frustrated gerbil owners simply give up and simply leave their gerbils in the cage to live out a wild existence. This is a really bad idea, as it makes it really stressful for your gerbil whenever he has to be handled – for example, if you bring him to the vet, or even if you need to move him to a container while you clean his cage. These situations are going to be tricky if your gerbil isn't tame. It is very sad to see a gerbil that never gets handled. So, make sure you keep going with the handling until your gerbil is calm enough to climb onto your hands voluntarily. It will be worth it.

Staying calm

Above all, you need to stay calm when handling your gerbil for the first time. One thing you could do if you're nervous is have a friend that has already tamed a gerbil to visit, and help with the process. Your gerbil needs to have positive experiences of being handled from the very start, or he will grow to associate your hands with a bad situation. So, make sure you're in a calm, positive frame of mind before you begin. Having a "can do" attitude is important.

How to handle nipping

If you have a particularly nippy little gerbil, you could wear gloves at the beginning if it makes you feel calmer. Once the gerbil gets used to the idea of being held and walking on your hands, you can phase out the gloves.

Try some treats

If you want your gerbil to feel distracted and maybe to associate handling with something rewarding, you can use treats at the very beginning. Some particularly tempting fruit or vegetables cut into tiny pieces should do the trick.

Choose somewhere with a soft landing

Before you take your gerbil out and handle him, you need to choose somewhere safe to do so. That means somewhere with a very soft landing, like the couch. If you stand up when handling your gerbil for the first time you are probably going to find he jumps out of your hands, or you get nipped and you drop him. You don't want him to have a huge fall when this happens. So, either sit on the carpet with your gerbil's cage just in front of you or choose a large couch to put the cage on and sit beside it. It's also a good idea to choose a room that is secure, with all windows and doors closed and no nooks and crannies for an escaped gerbil to hide away in. Make sure no one is going to walk into the room and interrupt you either – that could give you or your gerbil a fright, or if your gerbil is on the loose it could lead to him getting out of the room.

Step by step guide to handing

Here is a step-by-step guide to the very first time you try to handle your gerbil. Good luck!

1. Begin by getting your gerbil used to your smell. If you can put your hand inside the cage slowly without him flinching or hiding away, you are making progress. So, try to get to that stage before anything else. He should grow used to the idea that those giant hands of yours are nothing to be feared, and that they often bring gifts in the shape of delicious treats. Try spending an evening near the cage, putting your hand in at hourly intervals.

2. Get your gerbil to the stage where he is brave enough to approach your hands. This might take you a couple of hours, or it might take a day or two. It depends on the gerbil. Usually the best way to do this is to hold a small treat in the palm of your hand (inside the cage) and wait for curiosity to get the better of him. He will soon be at the stage where he crawls onto the palm of your hand

to get the treat. Stay calm and still when he does. Repeat this several times over a few hours so he gets the idea.

3. Once you're sure your gerbil is comfortable venturing onto your hand, you can progress to slowly moving the hand out of the cage when he is on it. This is much less stressful for him than being grabbed out of the blue. When you make a grab for a gerbil it seems like an attack from a predator, so try to avoid this practice wherever possible. Instead, you should let your gerbil make his way onto your hand in his own time, at least until he is properly tamed. Remember that we are trying to create only positive, rewarding experiences for your gerbil so that he gets more and more comfortable with being handled. Your gerbil might panic at this stage and jump off your hand back into the cage. If he does, don't worry. Just try again later.

4. When you can successfully move your hand (or hands) out of the cage with your gerbil on them, you can then start to properly handle him. If both parties are calm, this should go well. Gerbils like to be constantly on the move, so don't expect yours to sit perfectly still on your hand. Instead, give him the chance to walk from one hand to the other and keep rotating your hands like a treadmill, putting one hand in front of the other and so forth. Don't give your gerbil the chance to leap off – these are daring creatures and they will quite happily make the jump if they feel like it. Instead, always make sure your other hand is there in front of him so he can take his next steps. You will soon see him getting more and more active and faster on his legs. Gerbils tend to get more and more active the longer they exercise, so at the start of the handling session he will probably be slow and hesitant, but pretty soon he'll be racing along your hands.

5. Now it's time to get your gerbil used to being picked up, rather than simply using your hands as an elevator every time. To do this, put him in an enclosure with an open top but that he can't climb out of, like the bath or a box with very high sides. That way, you'll be able to practice picking him up rather than having to tempt him out of the awkwardly shaped cage every time. Put

a few distractions in the enclosure, like food and bedding, so he doesn't feel distressed. Then, simply use your two hands and cup them together. You are now going to scoop up your gerbil with your two hands, gently – not too quickly, or he will get a fright, but not so slowly that he has the chance to climb out of your hands before you've moved them off the ground.

6. Why use the scooping method? It is probably the most gentle and least invasive way to pick up a gerbil. Some people use more severe methods like pinching the scruff of the neck, or grabbing under the belly – these aren't necessary, and they aren't very nice for a fragile little gerbil to experience. NEVER pick up a gerbil by the tail – gerbils have the ability to shed the first layer of skin on their tails if they feel threatened, and this leaves the tail exposed to bacteria and injury. Gerbils aren't toys and they shouldn't be handled roughly or carelessly – they are fragile creatures that need respect from their owners. Once you've spent thirty minutes to an hour practising this scooping method, the gerbil should be at ease with it. There should never be any need to use a different method, unless your gerbil is having his teeth clipped or being examined by a vet.

A word about children and gerbils

If you have young children, please don't give them the responsibility of taming their own gerbil, especially if they haven't had a pet before. Children can be rough, and often get over-excited, forgetting that they are playing with a very real living thing that has delicate internal organs and can get frightened easily. Please tame each gerbil yourself before teaching your children how to handle it properly, and even then, please supervise your child until they are old enough to be trusted.

How to capture an escaped gerbil

It is an inevitable fact that someday, somehow, your gerbil is going to escape its cage or escape your grasp and run free somewhere in your house. When that happens, there are a few important things to do.

Alert everyone in the house that there is a gerbil on the loose. Gerbils are so tiny that people need to watch where they are stepping. Close all the windows and all the doors in the house. Each room should be sealed off to contain the gerbil, even if you're not sure which room he is in. Lock away any other pets immediately.

Now go to the room where you suspect your gerbil could be (if you don't know, simply follow these steps for each room one by one).

Spend a few minutes in the room sitting absolutely still and listening very carefully. When a gerbil is on the loose you can usually hear it eating carpet is a favourite activity, climbing curtains and even just running on the floorboards with its little feet can be heard. You might be lucky enough to catch a glimpse of him if you are vigilant enough.

Leave a particularly pungent smelling treat out in the centre of the room and sit nearby. Gerbils have an excellent sense of smell and it shouldn't be too long before yours comes running to see what tasty treat is there.

Once he's out in the open, you can drop a tea towel over him, a bucket or even a box. Then you can reach under it and pick him up. You can also try a long tube if you have one – gerbils love dark little hiding holes. Simply wait till he's entered the tube and then block the ends. If those methods fail, try setting up a humane trap and checking the trap first thing in the morning. Some escapees can take days or even weeks to be coaxed back into captivity, so don't give up!

Chapter 7:

What do gerbils eat?

Congratulations! You have come this far and you're now ready to start a daily care routine for your new little friends. This chapter will go through the kind of diet your gerbils need in order to keep them happy and healthy.

Feeding your gerbils

Once a day your little pet needs to be fed with fresh muesli (cereal) made specifically for gerbils, which you can buy from the pet shop. Make sure the muesli you buy is good quality, with plenty of different nuts, seeds and grains included. You will soon see that your gerbils have their favourite parts of the cereal, because the bits they don't like will be left behind!

Note: you should never feed your gerbils cereal or muesli that has been made for human consumption; this will be far too sugary and filled with ingredients your gerbils do not need. Stick to foods that have been produced specifically for gerbils.

Giving treats

In addition to his normal cereal, you can also add some treats to your gerbils' menu. It's very easy to find things in your fridge that a gerbil will eat (fruits, nuts and vegetables are always good ideas) so there should be no need to buy any of the processed, packaged gerbil treats you'll see in pet shops.

Treats should be given only every few days; you don't want to upset your gerbils' tummies by giving them too much fruit and veg in one go. Don't pile up the food bowl with treats, just give a few small pieces. Also bear in mind that some treats are going to be hoarded away in their burrows for later. You don't want this hoard of treats to build up and go stale. The RSPCA recommends scattering treats around your gerbil's cage (avoiding the corners he uses as toilet areas) in order to mimic the foraging they would naturally do in the wild.

Here are some treats your gerbils will probably love:
- Cucumber
- Carrot
- Apple
- Broccoli
- Pear
- Celery
- Blackberries
- Blueberries
- Banana
- Chicory
- Alfalfa
- Courgette

- Mange tout
- Green beans
- Cress
- Sweetcorn
- Sweet potato
- Turnip

Make sure all of the above treats are cut into tiny pieces that will be easy for your gerbils to eat. Also, wash everything thoroughly before-hand. Today's fruit and veg is treated with a lot of chemicals which could harm a tiny gerbil.

Protein for gerbils

Gerbils are omnivores and in the wild they would eat insects. Whilst we don't suggest you feed them insects, you can give your gerbils a little bit of protein about once a week in the form of low fat cottage cheese or cooked pieces of egg. Nuts are also a great source of protein, but gerbils can get ill if they are given too many fatty foods, so always feed these treats in moderation.

Foods that gerbils can't eat

Make sure everyone in your family knows that they can't feed your gerbils the following foods, as they are likely to make them quite sick:
- Lettuce which can cause liver problems
- Onion
- Raw kidney beans
- Raw potato and raw potato tops
- Tomato leaves
- Rhubarb and rhubarb leaves
- Human foods like chocolate

Food safety

Don't guess what your gerbils might be able to eat. Always check with your vet if you aren't sure.

Old food

Every day, you should do a quick scan of your gerbils' cage and nesting box and remove any food that is stale or has been there for too long. This will make sure your gerbils don't eat anything that makes them ill, and it will also make their home a more hygienic place to live.

Water

Gerbils can go long periods without water, as they evolved as creatures that lived in harsh desert conditions. However, those in captivity needs access to fresh water at all times. You should change the water in their bottle or bowl every day, even if you think it looks clean. Water that is left stagnant can go stale, and might also be a breeding ground for algae which is a green slimey substance that may harm your pets.

Supplements

There should be no need to give your gerbils vitamin supplements as long as you are feeding them a balanced, varied diet of muesli and fresh foods. The only time you might need to give extra vitamin and mineral supplements is if your gerbils fall ill and your vet has advised you to. Giving large amounts of supplements can throw a gerbil's system out of balance and may even make them feel worse. So, only give these under the direction of your vet.

Chapter 8:

Gerbil health

Now that you're a fully-fledged hamster owner, it's time to familiarise yourself with hamster health in general. It's important to know the signs of illness in hamsters and also to know what is and isn't healthy – it could save you a trip to the vet some day. This chapter will give you the facts you need to know.

Healthy hamster checklist

Every time you handle your hamster, do a quick health check to make sure he is well and thriving. Here is a check list to go through:

- Eyes are bright, clear and alert
- Coat is healthy, glossy with no bald patches
- Skin has no sores, scaly patches or inflammation
- Body has no unusual lumps or bumps
- Hamster has not lost weight (bones will be easier to feel if so)
- Breathing is easy, with no wheezes or sneezes
- No discharge coming from the rear end, nose or eyes
- Ears are clean and clear of debris
- Movement is fluid with no limping or signs of pain
- Behaviour is normal, with no odd changes

Knowing the signs of illness

A good hamster owner knows the classic signs of illness, and is always vigilant for any of the following signs that something is wrong:
-
- Loss of appetite – food is left unfinished or untouched
- Excessive drinking from the water bottle (hamsters don't usually drink too much)
- Lethargy and listlessness when the hamster is normally active and

alert
- Hamster stays in the nesting box at times when it would usually be out and about
- Dull or sunken eyes
- Sitting in a hunched position rather than relaxed posture, which is a sign of pain
- Diarrhoea, or sticky, wet faeces which sometimes get matted in the fur
- Discharge coming from the nose, eyes or rear end
- Sneezing, coughing or wheezing
- A hard, swollen tummy
- Signs of injury, such as trailing a limb or limping
- Difficulty walking or seeming off-balance
- Scratching a lot on the same area of skin
- Abnormal bumps or lumps on the body
- Behavioural changes, such as suddenly not wanting to be handled, being unusually aggressive, or simply sleeping around the clock instead of waking up to exercise

Knowing when to visit the vet

The lists above should be very helpful in knowing whether to take your hamster to the vet. If you spot any of the above symptoms, you should book a vet's appointment as soon as you can.

Hamsters are so small and they don't make any noise, so hamster owners need to be very observant for signs of ill health that could easily go unnoticed. In particular, if you have children who normally handle your hamster, you should teach them about the signs above and what to look for.

Once a week, you should ask to look over the hamster yourself just to make sure he is healthy.

Common hamster diseases

In addition to knowing the signs of ill-health, you may want to be aware of the following common hamster illnesses:

Every experienced hamster owner knows that wet tail can be very contagious. As the name suggests, this infection can cause watery faeces which cause the fur around the tail and bottom to feel wet. If you notice this in your hamster you should immediately separate him from any other hamsters in the group, and take him to the vet.

To be safe, if you keep a group of hamsters then they should all be seen by the vet to be sure. Normally though, wet tail affects the Golden or Syrian hamster more, and these hamsters aren't kept in groups. Vets usually treat this condition with antibiotics and fluids (your hamster may become easily dehydrated with diarrhoea). If caught early the condition can be treated and cured, but in more severe cases it can be fatal.

Bald patches and fur loss

If your hamster suddenly seems to have patches of fur missing, there could be a problem. Firstly, it could be that your hamster has mites, which are a tiny parasite that causes itching and a lot of stress. Your hamster will rub his body against the sides of the cage and will be persistently scratching and biting at the affected areas, causing the fur to fall out. Mites need to be treated by a vet as they cause your hamster a lot of discomfort and are also contagious between pets. So, the bedding and cage of a hamster with mites will need to be cleaned and disinfected thoroughly to kill all the mites.

You will need to do this very regularly whilst your hamster is being treated. Topical sprays are normally used, and if you have a group of hamsters the whole colony will need to be treated. Mange is another condition caused by mites, usually in the hamster's ears. They can cause an allergic reaction in your hamster leading to scabs and sores on the fur – a very sore and uncomfortable condition for your little pet. Creams, oral medications and injections can be used to kill off the mange, and any sores can be soothed with topical treatments.

Other causes of fur loss can be malnutrition, stress or fighting between hamsters that live in groups. Your vet should be able to make a proper diagnosis on examining your hamster.

Colds

Hamsters can catch colds from time to time, especially if they live in a cage that is kept somewhere damp or draughty. They can also catch colds from humans, so if you are ill, please don't handle your hamster until you are better! Avoid giving your hamster baths as this, too, can cause him to catch cold. Wheezing, sneezing and wet noses are all signs of a cold.

Keep your hamster somewhere warm and cosy and feed him some soft, vitamin C rich foods. If your hamster's cold seems severe you should take him to the vet as a cold can quickly develop into pneumonia in small creatures.

Red urine

Reddish coloured urine isn't always a sign of illness. Sometimes, it's caused by artificial dyes in your hamster's food. To be sure, you should change your hamster's diet and if the red urine doesn't go away, you will need to take him to the vet. Other causes of reddish urine include bladder stones, or an infection in the uterus called pyometra.

Pyometra

This infection of the uterus can be life threatening. It starts with bloody discharge and progresses over time until the hamster's uterus or abdomen swells to an abnormal size. Vet treatment should be sought as soon as possible.

Overgrown teeth

A very common problem that happens to hamsters is that their teeth grow so long that they can no longer eat. Often these hamsters haven't been given anything to chew on (such as a piece of wood or a mineral stone) that will file down the teeth. You might not notice anything is wrong until your hamster begins to lose weight and ignore much of the food in its bowl. This is because the teeth have made it too difficult to eat. A quick trip to the vet will confirm this, and your vet will clip your hamster's teeth back so that he can eat again. He may show you how to clip the teeth yourself at home, if you are confident enough.

Impacted pouches

Sometimes your hamster gets carried away and will try to store something in his pouches that really isn't suitable. Bedding is one common culprit. The result is that the item gets lodged in the pouch and the pouch becomes impacted. If you've noticed a familiar bulge in one of your hamster's pouches that stays there for more than a couple of days, there may be something stuck in the pouch that needs to be removed by the vet.

Conjunctivitis

If your hamster develops an allergy to his bedding, or if a tiny piece of debris gets in his eyes, he may show signs of conjunctivitis where the eye is red, inflamed and irritated. There may be discharge, and the hamster will rub at its eyes due to the irritation. Drops are available to treat these issues, and you should also look at changing your hamster's bedding if you think it might be causing an allergy. Sawdust is a common issue as the tiny particles of dust can easily get into the eyes.

Poisoning

If your hamster has come into contact with anything toxic, or he has accidentally eaten something harmful, he needs to go to the vet. Some substances which are toxic to hamsters include:

- Mouse or rodent poison
- Foxglove plants
- Chocolate
- Ivy

- Rhubarb and rhubarb leaves
- Oleander

Hibernation

In the wild, some hamsters will hibernate to get them through the harsh winters. Hibernation is when the animal goes into a very deep sleep and many of the usual bodily functions are put on hold, for example they will only wake up very occasionally to feed. Hamsters in captivity don't need to hibernate and usually they will not.

However, if they are particularly sensitive to the cold or are accidentally kept somewhere with no heating (not advisable under any circumstances!) they may go into hibernation as a natural reaction. If you believe your hamster is in hibernation, there is no need to disturb it (this might cause unnecessary stress). Simply make sure the room is nice and warm and there is plenty of fresh food and water left out for when he wakes. If the room gets warmer, he will wake up naturally in his own time.

Using the checklist

This list of hamster health issues isn't exhaustive, so don't rely on evidence mentioned here as a sign that you should visit the vet. In reality, anything odd or unusual (for example those symptoms listed in the checklist at the beginning of this chapter) should be cause for concern.

The good thing is hamster health care is usually not too expensive – these little animals are a lot cheaper to care for than dogs and cats. So you shouldn't feel worried about visiting the vet, even if it is for something minor. The chances are, your vet will be glad to see someone who takes such a keen, proactive interest in their pet's health.

Chapter 9:
Gerbil FAQs

This chapter will deal with some of your most commonly asked questions on keeping gerbils. You can keep this book and refer to it throughout your career as a gerbil enthusiast. It may come in very handy.

How often should I clean out my gerbil's cage? And how should I do it?

You should do a full clean of your gerbils' cage at least once a week. Never leave it to the stage where it gets smelly, or where there are faeces everywhere. Your little gerbils rely on you to keep their home clean and they will be very unhappy and unhealthy if left somewhere dirty. Some tips for cleaning out your gerbils' cage include:

Find somewhere safe to put your gerbils while you're cleaning the cage. Bathtubs are often a good idea because your gerbils can't climb out of them.

Start by emptying all of the substrate out of the base of the cage into a bin bag. Then, empty out all of the bedding and old food from the nesting box. Disinfect the walls and base of the tank, the wheel and the food bowl, as well as the nesting box. Some cleaning solution in a bucket of hot water and a few wet cloths should do the trick. Clean the base until no trace of dirt or debris remains.

Rinse everything you have just washed in fresh water, so that there is no trace of disinfectant left behind (it contains harmful chemicals which could affect your gerbils). Dry everything thoroughly. Then, put down a fresh layer of paper in the bottom of the tank, and cover it with several inches of substrate for burrowing. Put new bedding into the clean, dry nesting box and replace the clean food bowl with fresh food. Once the cage is back together, your gerbils can be put back into their lovely clean home.

How do I tell if a gerbil is male or female?

In adult gerbils, a female has noticeable nipples on the underside of her tummy. In males, there will be a bulge under the tail where the testes are located. In younger gerbils, simply hold the tail up and look at the gerbil's rear end. Female gerbils have two little holes (one for pee and one for poo) which are quite close together, whereas in males the holes are noticeably further apart.

Can I give my gerbils a bath? How else can I keep them clean?

No, you should never give your gerbils a bath. This would be too stressful and they might catch a cold from it, which could be life threatening. If your gerbil has something dirty matted in his fur, you can use a toothbrush to get it out, or you can simply clip away the soiled fur. For keeping the fur clean, you can give your gerbils a dust bath once every few days by placing a little tray of chinchilla dust in their tank. Be sure to take it away after they have used it, or it may soon become a toilet area!

Can I toilet train my gerbil?

Believe it or not, some owners manage to successfully train their gerbils to pee in a particular spot in their cages. A little tray of substrate is a good thing to try, or even just a shallow little box in the corner of the cage, so that the rest of the cage stays clean and dry. Some gerbils like a small jam jar left on its side. Fill the toilet tray with some sawdust that has already been peed on and a couple of faeces. With a bit of luck, your gerbil will soon get the idea that this is where the toilet is. Gerbils are very clean animals and usually go to the toilet in one corner of the cage anyway. This way, you can actually remove the soiled tray and replace it throughout the week, so that there is no smell in the cage between the weekly clean out.

I've heard gerbils can be trained to do tricks. Is this true?

Yes, some gerbil owners manage to teach their gerbils tricks like coming when they are called, begging for food and staying put. This is done with a technique called positive reinforcement, where the gerbil is rewarded with a treat when it behaves in the right way.

Can I let my gerbil run around the house?

You can let your gerbil run free as long as it's in a safe, secured room with the doors and windows closed. All potential hazards should be out of the way, for example cables which could be chewed, or unfamiliar house plants which your gerbil might try to eat. Don't attempt to let your gerbil run free until he is fully tamed or you will have a real problem catching him again. Bear in mind that once your gerbil gets a taste for freedom he will want to be out running around all of the time.

Conclusion

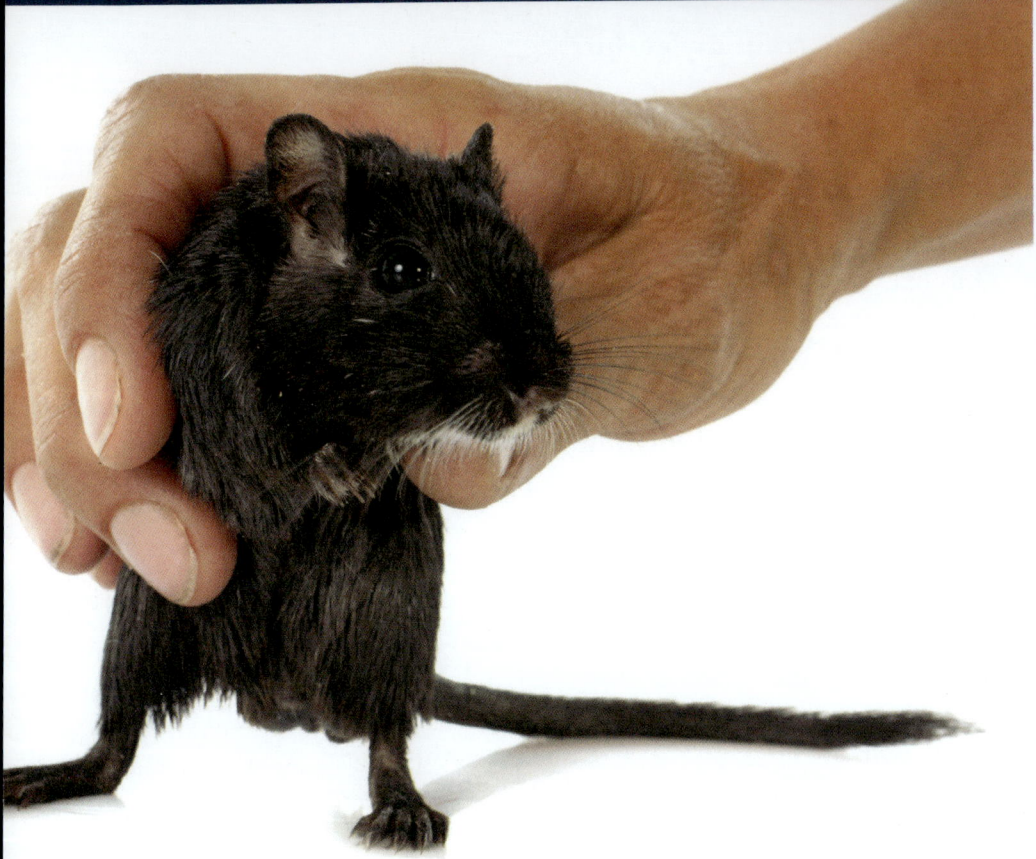

We hope you've enjoyed this book and that you have learnt enough about gerbils to be a responsible, conscientious gerbil owner. Becoming the owner of one of these charismatic creatures is a very rewarding experience, and you are going to have a lot of fun in the days and months to come. You'll see for yourself how these cheeky and funny little pets managed to charm their way out of laboratories and into people's homes and families. May you and your gerbil have many happy times together!

Want to know more about looking after your pet?

The writer of this book, Dr. Gordon Roberts, is a veterinarian and owns a total of eight animal hospitals around the UK. He believes that the key to a healthy, happy pet is preventative care, which is only possible when pet owners take the initiative to educate themselves about their animals. As a result, Gordon has written dozens of useful reports on pet care in order to share his years of experience with discerning pet owners. As a thank you for purchasing this book, you can browse and download his specialist reports completely free of charge! You'll learn all sorts of useful information about how to spot possible health conditions early on, and how to make preventative care for your pet a priority, helping you save time and money on visits to the vet later on. To view and download these bonus reports, simply visit Gordon's website at: http://drgordonroberts.com/freereportsdownload/.

Best wishes,
Gordon

35882876R00026

Printed in Great Britain
by Amazon